PROFIT FROM YOUR UNIQUENESS

Get insights to effectively leverage your uniqueness in business.

OPEYEMI ABE

Copyright © 2020 by Opeyemi Abe

oabe@opeyemiabe.com
All Rights Reserved.

Edited by;
Nkem Menkiti, nkemmenkiti@gmail.com

No part of this document may be used, shared, or reproduced by any means, graphic, electronic, mechanical, including photocopy, recording, taping, or other – except for brief quotations in critical reviews or articles, without the prior written permission of the publisher.

DEDICATION

I dedicate this book to my lovely wife and backbone, Raliat Abe. Thank you for the wonderful partnership over the years.

And to all members of the Marketplace Champions Group, who have given me the opportunity to train and coach them, and also benefit from their support. I appreciate you all.

ACKNOWLEDGMENT

Relationship plays a major role in life and I have benefited from it in the course of writing, producing, and publishing this book. A number of people have played different roles to bring this book to life. I may not be able to mention all their names but my special appreciation goes to Oba Boniface Omozuapo for his feedbacks in the course of writing the book, Nkem Menkiti for the editing, sometimes at very short notice. Also Anthonia Oraeki, a member of Marketplace Champions Group and a great supporter, Favour Ajayi for the formatting and e-book creation, Mr. Yinka Obikanye, and my dear sister Tunrayo Ahenmokhai of Lagos House Wife for their encouragement and immense support. And of course my lovely wife, Raliat Abe, for the insightful discussions we had while writing the book.

I thank Almighty God for giving me the wisdom and grace to write this book. I am grateful.

TESTIMONIALS

Great work and thought provoking! It is a book that will make people look more inwards in search of creative and innovative solutions.

OBA BONIFACE OMOZUAPO
Managing Director/CEO
De Ambassadors Advisory & Investment Ltd

This book is simply amazing and a must have for every entrepreneur. It contains some tested and trusted principles that will position you to profit from maximizing your innate potentials and God-given talents. It is a worthwhile read with well explained concepts. I have no doubt that whoever picks it up will easily understand and apply the principles explained in the book.

NKEM MENKITI
LN Editorial Services

CONTENTS

Introduction 7

Chapter 1
You are Unique 10

Chapter 2
I like myself 22

Chapter 3
People need your solution 30

Chapter 4
Your uniqueness in business 35

Chapter 5
Your uniqueness is in their minds 44

Chapter 6
Know your market 50

Chapter 7
Developing your USP 58

Chapter 8
From Personal to Corporate 69

Chapter 9
From innate virtue to Business Value 84

Chapter 10
Promoting your USP 93

Chapter 11
Crafting your USP in the mind 98

Chapter 12
There is no competition 104

Chapter 13
Shine your light 120

INTRODUCTION

Many markets and industries are plagued by sameness; this is a condition where virtually all companies in a particular sector offer the same products and services, and target the same set of customers. Competitors in such markets are quick to imitate newly launched products such that there will be multiple nomenclatures for the same kind of service or products because they are offered and sold by different companies.

Consumers can hardly tell the difference between competing products and some simply make their purchase decisions based on price or other less compelling factors.

Many small business owners find themselves in this scenario, including new entrants in their markets; and a lot of them adjust to the situation either because they are unwilling to pay the price of innovative thinking, or are afraid of upsetting the status quo because they doubt their capacity to make a difference. Several business owners have stopped listening to their creative voices and inspiration to develop unique solutions for their markets.

The implication of this is that many consumers are not well served, because people have diverse needs but the available businesses are offering them very limited options. Several small businesses are also unable to carve a niche for their companies or attract their own markets.

The solution is for small business owners to start listening more to their intuition, identifying their unique strengths and attributes, and developing them into a competitive edge and Unique Selling Proposition. With that they can establish a clear difference between their businesses and those of the competition, develop a loyal market base, and also become more profitable.

That is why this book was written. It offers a guide for small business owners who want to differentiate their businesses and stand out in their markets. The first few chapters focuses on the business owners and how they can identify and develop their uniqueness, while the subsequent chapters provide steps on how to bring their uniqueness to bear in their businesses and stand out profitably in their market.

Each chapter is followed by statements and questions to help the reader reflect and apply the lessons from it. The book is designed to help you take the right action that will guarantee you results.

Consumers are looking for innovation and variety, not sameness; and we need more small businesses to embark on deliberate innovation and differentiation strategies so they can serve their markets and also themselves much better.

I hope this book guides and inspires you to do that well.

CHAPTER 1

YOU ARE UNIQUE

"You are the only you God made....God made you and broke the mold"

-Max Lucado

YOU ARE UNIQUE

You may have heard it said before that all human beings are different, and that each person is unique; but have you really given that statement a good thought?

Scientists have since discovered that no two human beings are genetically identical; a study conducted by scientists at the University of Alabama at Birmingham and a couple of other Universities years ago further attested to the fact that even identical twins do not share the same DNA. Research over the years has revealed more characteristics that are innate in every human being, and both security and technology companies use them for personal identification and authentication;

examples are the finger print, Iris, and the voice. There are many more traits in the human body, soul, and spirit that uniquely differentiate one person from another.

A major part of the beauty of creation is the uniqueness of each person and animal. According to the Federation Cynologique Internationale (FCI) the world governing body of dog breeds, there are about 340 breeds of dogs with multiple variants for each, and more breeds are still being discovered. There are over 4,000 species of snails discovered so far, including different kinds of sea snails and fresh water snails. This fact applies to all animals, birds, insects, and plants. We live in a world of diversity and we all should appreciate that fact.

I often find it interesting when I observe the contrast in my two daughters; one is highly extroverted, friendly, and emotional, while the other is a lot more reserved, logical, observant, and less socially inclined. One day my first daughter saw a wall gecko in her room and quickly ran out screaming "Daddy, there is a lizard in the room!" The younger sister who was sitting in the living room suddenly stood up and said "where is the lizard, show me let me chase it out!" I was amazed watching a three year old girl act that way. That was instinctive, and markedly different from her sister's disposition.

Many of us can attest to the fact that even though we grew up with our siblings in the same environment there is a huge contrast between us in terms of personality, interests, values, life goals, and other attributes. Even though our cultural backgrounds, education, and other life experiences can have an influence on how we turn out, we still have inherent qualities that are unique to us and significantly determine how we lead our lives.

Each of us bring our uniqueness to bear as we work, that is why you can have two accountants, singers, doctors, engineers, or comedians perform the same tasks but produce different experiences, impacts, and outcomes.

I once had an encounter with two sales representatives from the same company; both of them were very professional in their approach, and they made effort to connect with me. I however noticed that one was more compassionate, kind, and supportive; he was more of a feeler, while the other connected with me intellectually, he engaged me in my area of interest, and was a very persuasive communicator. Both of them were great sales people, but each one stood out with their different strengths and talents.

DISCOVERING YOUR DIFFERENCE

The important thing is not just that we are different, we also need to discover our unique differences. The above statement is very significant because instead of trying to make ourselves different by acquiring some new attributes and competences, we can simply groom what is inherently ours.

There is so much you need to discover about yourself, if you have not; these includes your personal beliefs, values, vision, talents, passion, personality, suitable career path, strengths, and weaknesses.

Discovering yourself is important because it enables you to

deliberately live a more fulfilling life. If you discover your passion and values, for instance, you can deliberately organize your work life around the things you value and are passionate about, and that will make you a happier person. When you know your strengths and inherent talents you can structure your life to continuously hone them through practice and become outstanding in your area of giftedness. What about when you realize your weaknesses? That knowledge can help you know where to seek help and minimize the effect of your weaknesses on your performance. Discovering your uniqueness will help you to manage your life better to achieve success.

How to discover your uniqueness

Several Personality and value discovery tests are available and easily accessible online, results from these tests can give you better understanding about your person. Anytime I advise people on self-discovery I introduce them to the 4P Framework which I came up with based on my study and experience in the area of purpose discovery.

The 4Ps are Passion, Potential, Pain, and Priorities.

1. **Passion:** This has to do with what you love and enjoy doing. Passion is that energy that keeps you going, and fills you with excitement and happiness. It often comes when you are doing something that connects with your soul and very essence, and fills you with a sense that you are doing something meaningful, that really matters. How do you know what you are passionate about? When you are doing it, the work itself is a reward for you. You find so much joy and satisfaction doing it, when you get paid or recognized for it, it becomes an extra reward. One of the greatest secrets of the world's successful people is simply this – they love what they do.

2. **Potential:** Your potential is what you are capable of doing. It is what you do well naturally, sometimes it even surprises you how you get the inspiration and have the instinct to do it well.

   Your potential reveals your natural wiring, talents, and gifts. Have you seen people who naturally sing so well without going to any music school? And someone skilled in selling and running a business without having a business degree or training? They simply became good by following their instincts and improving through consistent practice.

One of the ways you know your potential is from people's feedback. People notice what you are good at, especially people who are close to you. Whenever you display that ability people are impressed, and sometimes even you are impressed at your results. If you focus on what you are naturally good at you will have the support of your natural instincts and inspiration to achieve great results in less time and with considerably little effort.

3. **Pain:** Pain has to do with what concerns or grieves you; what you wish you could change in the world. Everyone has something that bothers them, something they would want to see change in the world; and it signifies what they should spend their time doing. If you want to make impact in the lives of others and in this world you must work in an area you feel a compelling need to intervene in. A major reason why Mandela was successful in the Apartheid struggle was because he was grieved by the injustice meted out to his kinsmen and fellow black South Africans. A major reason Oprah Winfrey is so successful with her Talk Show is her compassion for people and their pains, which could be traced to her own childhood trauma.

Bill Gates wanted as many people as possible to have access to computers; the founders of Google had a compelling need to make information universally accessible, and that was a driving force for them.

What is the compelling need that you have? What problem are you drawn to? What pain do you want to alleviate for others? Life's most persistent question is "what are you doing for others?" You can find what you should be doing through the pain you feel.

When you work in the areas you have a compelling need to make a difference, which may be education, social justice, fashion, personal development, business, or health etc, you are naturally fuelled and driven from your soul to achieve success in them.

4. **Priorities:** Your priorities represent your values, which are simply the things that are important to you in life. Your values are unique to you. What is important to you may not be important to another person, and often times that is not a bad thing at all.

    Your personal values can also be informed by your family background, religious affiliation, friends, life experiences etc. Examples of values include accountability, punctuality, respect, integrity, service, loyalty, security, generosity, friendliness, honesty, hard-work, family, flexibility, excellence, responsibility, and lots more. For more on values you can check Scot Jeffrey's write-up titled "Guide: How to discover your core values", (2018); Patrick Buggy's article on "5 Steps to Define your core values: A compass for navigating life decisions" (mindfulambition.net/author/Patrick-j-buggy/).

An individual who has punctuality as a strong personal value will hate attending meetings or appointments late, and will often be displeased at those who come late for an appointment. People who value excellence want things always on point, they can sometimes display perfectionist tendencies too. If these kind of people work in an office that does not value timeliness or paying attention to details, they are unlikely to find the place appealing.

What you need is to discover your values and endeavor to live your life consistent with them so you can be more productive and fulfilled.

REFLECT & APPLY:

1. Have you discovered your uniqueness? If not, you can go through this chapter again, and meditatively assess yourself. Ask people who are close to you for clues about your unique personality, talents, passion, values.

   _____
   _____
   _____

2. Go through some of the tests recommended, including Kolbe Personality Test (www.kolbe.com), Tom Rath, StrengthsFinder 2.0 (www.amazon.com/StrengthsFinder 2.0); they will give you a clue to your unique strengths.

   _____
   _____
   _____

3. Start making efforts to apply yourself and practice in your area of strength. The more you practice, the more knowledge you gain about yourself, and the more proficient you become in your area of strength.

_____

_____

_____

CHAPTER 2

I LIKE MYSELF

"No one is you, and that is your power"

-Dave Grohl

I LIKE MYSELF

As humans we are not the architects of our beings; we are God's creation and our uniqueness is ingrained in our nature. As I mentioned in the previous chapter, there are a lot of things that are natural to us, including our DNA, our Iris, finger print etc. You also did not choose your gender, natural skin colour, personality, talents, and passions. It is however very important that you accept yourself.

DESIRING ANOTHER LIFE

While I was in Secondary School I had a classmate named Grace, who often said if she could come back to the earth a second time she would prefer to come as a male, and not female. According to her, males are accorded more privileges in our world. But the truth is that even if she comes to the world a second time she still wouldn't be the one to determine her gender. These things are designed by God. Our role is to learn to appreciate who we really are, and embrace our uniqueness.

Why do some girls want to become boys? Why do some black Africans want to become white? Why do some skinny people want to become plump and vice versa? Because they simply have not accepted themselves the way they were originally created. The first step towards expressing your unique self and becoming your best is to like yourself.

You need to like and accept yourself; I mean the way you were created – spirit, soul, and body, except you have a major deformity that needs to be corrected. Your self-improvement efforts should be centered on developing your natural potential and not altering your nature.

When you take the time and effort to discover yourself and your unique purpose you will find that you are actually wonderful the way you are. You need to list out all the strengths and good attributes you have, and read them to yourself often. Some of you will need to say to yourself regularly "I like myself!" You are going to spend a great deal of time with yourself, so you can as well fall in love with you. Love yourself.

I know people who have some unique talents but do not admire them, rather they desire other talents that they do not have.

We once had a domestic help who was very gifted in cooking; she instinctively knew how to develop recipes and combine items to make a good meal. She later got a job in a restaurant and within a short time she became one of their very outstanding cooks. This lady however preferred a totally different career because of the fame and fortune associated with it. She despised what she was naturally good at to seek for fame outside her gift zone. It is a typical example of someone not liking and embracing their uniqueness.

The moment you accept your natural talents, passion, and personality you set yourself up for a more fulfilling life.

THE FLOW STATE

Flow is a psychological state you experience when you are deeply engaged in work that you are passionate about and which connects with your essence. When you are in this state you lose sense of time, you enjoy support from your natural instincts and get inspiration that helps you achieve a high level of performance in your work. Mihaly Csikszentmihalyi, an American psychologist gave the concept the name, and it has since been popularized. Steven Kotler is one of the leading teachers of this concept, and he explains the direct connection between flow states and peak performance of human beings. One major way to experience flow is to focus intensely, immerse yourself in the activity you are engaged in, and remove distractions; it triggers inspiration and knowledge from your subconscious mind. Your passion is however important in triggering flow states for you, because you pay more attention to things that you are passionate about.

In this (flow) state you are not only at your creative best but also at rest, energized, and excited. Some of the greatest authors, scientists, athletes, engineers, musicians, and entrepreneurs that you know or admire experience this state consistently. An example is the basketball legend, Michael Jordan, who experiences flow states often when he is playing the game. Isaac Newton was also a man who often experienced this state while carrying out experiments in the lab.

Research has shown that those who constantly visit this state perform exceptionally in their fields; they are often among the best in their profession. There is a flow state at the heart of every outstanding achievement in life.

Another fact from research is that flow is fundamental to your wellbeing and overall satisfaction in life. If you want to continuously enjoy this state of relaxed, creative, high performance you have to embrace your passion, gifts, and talents, develop them and practice them regularly. Flow is at its best when you are in your natural elements. Don't be envious of other people's talents. Embrace your own, cultivate it, and aim to become the best in it. Aim to express your full potential.

REFLECT & APPLY:

1. Have you embraced who you are and become comfortable with your uniqueness?

   _____
   _____
   _____

2. What two steps can you take from today to start appreciating your unique personality, talents, and passions more?

   _____
   _____
   _____

CHAPTER 3

PEOPLE NEED YOUR SOLUTION

"Could you be the one your market is waiting for?"
-Unknown

PEOPLE NEED YOUR SOLUTION

When you discover and express your unique strengths and qualities you become a solution to some people's problems. People have unique needs they want to meet, and there are people you are uniquely designed to be a solution to their problems. As different as we are in this world is how different the solutions we offer to people. I believe everyone can be a solution provider; you have a passion to do something, there are aspects of human life, our society, or the earth that are of great concern to you and when you take the time to reflect and dig deep into your soul, you will find a cause to live for. There is a peculiar problem you are attracted to; your combination of talents, passion, and personality adds up to provide specific value to others, and there are people out there who need your value, you just need to shine your light to attract them.

Some of the famous people we admire started by giving expression to their unique talents or abilities and offered them as solutions to other people's and organisation's problems.

Bill Gates of Microsoft had an uncanny ability to write computer programmes. He did not only practice the skill, he used it to solve problems for organisations. Steve Jobs brought revolution to the personal computer and mobile phone industry by consistently using his talent for design and inventions to proffer solutions to the society. Asa, a Nigerian Singer and song writer, is one of the artists who sings a unique genre of music which has inspired many. She got her inspiration from a combination of American, Nigerian, and African soul classics. Her style of music was neither popular, nor conventional, but she gave it expression all the same, and it has gained acceptance among her favourite audience across the world.

John Bramblitt, is a blind painter of American origin who is currently ranked the number one blind painter in the world. His works have sold in over 20 different countries. He is also the author of the award winning book "Shouting in the dark".

After falling into depression for a long time due to the loss of his eyesight at the age of 30, he found his passion and salvation in painting. He gave it expression, and has since offered his gift as a solution to his market and fans across the world who really love his style of painting.

You have a solution embedded in you, and you will be surprised to know that there are people waiting for you to give your uniqueness an expression so they can find the answer to their needs in you. Your audience is looking for you; you need to shine your light for them to find you. If you don't shine your light they cannot come to you.

REFLECT & APPLY:

1. How can you start putting your strengths and talents to use to add value to other people?

   _____
   _____
   _____

2. What steps can you take to make your talents commercially viable?

   _____
   _____
   _____

CHAPTER 4

YOUR UNIQUENESS IN BUSINESS

"Don't just say what you do well, show what you do differently"

-Jack Hanson

YOUR UNIQUENESS IN BUSINESS

Being unique also pays off in business, and it can help you succeed in your market. When all brands look alike in the marketplace they appear as a commodity to the customer; products and services all look and feel the same such that the customer does not have a reason to patronize a particular brand. Such a market suffers from sameness.

In the olden days, before the advent of brands, different merchants came to the market with similar goods and it was difficult for buyers to differentiate among the goods; but even at that time many merchants wanted their products to be distinguished from other similar commodities in the market, and that desire led to branding.

Branding is said to have begun with ancient Egyptians who traded in livestock. They branded their livestock by means of a distinctive symbol burned into their animal's skin with a hot iron. That was their way of making their livestock (products) easily identifiable and also preferred by consumers in the open market. So the desire to be identified, and to stand out in the market has always been among business people.

By branding their products it becomes easy for customers who have met with them before to easily identify their products, and they could attract other customers to their corner as well. While our discourse here is not on branding, it is however on a very similar and related subject.

As an entrepreneur in today's world of business you miss a lot if you do not have a unique identity in the customers' minds; you can lose sales, profit, and your market position. It is the need to achieve this that led to the invention of Unique Selling Proposition. The term was coined in the early 1940s by Rosser Reeves, an American Advertising executive, but the concept had long been practiced by businesses in one form or another.

WHAT IS UNIQUE SELLING PROPOSITION?

Unique Selling Proposition (or Unique Selling Point) is that factor or consideration that makes your business, product, or service different from or better than that of the competition. It is a unique benefit exhibited by your business, product, or service that makes it stand out from competitors'. Your USP is very effective if it clearly differentiates your business from the competition in the minds of customers.

Theodore Levitt, a professor at Harvard Business School, once said "Differentiation is one of the most important strategic and tactical activities which companies must constantly engage"; that is very true, and a good USP is an effective tool to help you achieve differentiation in your market.

A Scenario;

If you are in business, selling a product or providing a service, and you happen to be the only one in that kind of business, you don't need to stand out. Everyone must come to you to have the product because they cannot get it elsewhere. All you may need to do is create more awareness, and let people know what you do. Customers will be attracted and keep coming to you because you are the ONLY one offering the service.

But in a competitive environment, you need to STAND OUT. You do not want your business and products to be seen as a commodity.

You know what that means? If customers view your business or product as a commodity they consider it as common, and do not see any significant difference between your business and that of your competitors. There is nothing special to make them choose your business over that of your competitors.

It's like going to a shopping complex where several stores sell similar clothes, electronics, or furniture etc, you often don't have a preferred company or brand in mind when going there. So, you can enter any store to buy what you want, with price being your major or only consideration. You may just be interested in going for the most affordable of similar items. I do not believe you want your business to be or remain at the level of commodity. You should aim higher than that.

Benefits of having a USP

Those who have successfully built a USP for their businesses enjoy some advantages, such as;

1. **Customer Loyalty:** You know what that implies? Customers will give your products very strong consideration. They will also be willing to pay higher for your products and services because your product is preferred.

2. **Selling becomes easier:** You get regular customer patronage without much effort on your part because customers are already sold on your product, service, or business.

3. **Improved revenue:** When your Unique Selling Proposition is very clear, known, and acceptable to prospects you will attract majority of your market. Those who need the special benefit you offer will come to you and your sales

revenue will soar.

I have found that customers intrinsically yearn for variety in the market space and many want to see differences in product types that offer them a choice. Customers do not like sameness in the market, because, really, consumers are different in their desires, needs, and aspirations. As a business owner, you will do well to stay away from SAMENESS in the market place; avoid imitation as much as possible and offer uniqueness to your market.

A GOOD USP STOOD THEM OUT

What is the Unique Selling Point of iPhones? What is that of Toyota? What about KFC Restaurant? What special benefit do you get from these products and businesses that their competitors do not offer you?

Apple iPhones offer its users productivity and class. Many of the people who buy iPhones like them because of the speed and responsiveness of the device software; it offers several user friendly features that make users enjoy the ease of achieving several things like watching videos, listening to music, downloading Applications, chatting, streaming, and networking with other devices using the phone technology. More importantly iPhones are marketed as a device of class, for the select few who want to be unique in the world, and it is given the physical aesthetics and feel that conveys this message to buyers. Many consumers of iPhones and other Apple products enjoy this feeling.

Toyota is popularly known for its durability, engine performance, and affordability. Users of Toyota products attest to the ease of maintenance as well as its functionality. Users of competitive products like Honda brands enjoy the design, aesthetics, and interiors of their cars, but they recognize Toyota for its functionality and durability.

When KFC started several years ago, it gained a loyal customer base because of the unique taste of its chicken which customers could not get anywhere else. Their chicken was both spicy and tasty and that stood their products out in their market.

An effectively crafted USP will stand your business out and give it a special place in your market.

REFLECT & APPLY:

What is the USP of your own product, service, or business? Why will customers choose your business over others?

_____
_____
_____

CHAPTER 5

YOUR UNIQUENESS IS IN THEIR MINDS

"Apple wants to reach your heart instead of your wallet."

-Carmine Gallo

YOUR UNIQUENESS IS IN THEIR MINDS

It was 1am on a September morning, there was a long queue of people waiting expectantly, at the same time there were others on camp beds sleeping under thick blankets. Some people were actually sleeping on the bare floor; one man was seen fast asleep covering himself with a garbage bag. Many people had come from different parts of town and even the world and spent over thirteen days sleeping outside the Apple store in the USA, all of them waiting earnestly for the release of iPhone 5s. It was the same scenario in London, Australia, and Asia at Apple stores. Customers and fans in large numbers were queuing up, with many defying the very cold weather, just to be the first to get their hands on the latest iPhone. The customers did not mind the fact that the phone did not come cheap either. They had been sold on the unique value of Apple products, particularly the iPhone.

Apple iPhones symbolized good taste and sophisticated design. That was a unique selling point that Apple's competitors could not match. Apple's USP was well ingrained in the minds of their customers. The company had done a good job of successfully positioning their products in the minds and hearts of their market, and that guaranteed them massive sales and loyal patronage beyond reasonable levels.

It is not enough for your products to have some special features and attributes, the customer must know and appreciate these attributes, and view them as exclusive to your company.

Ultimately your USP resides in the minds of the customers; they are the ones who view your products as special and unique or not. Your company adverts, promotions, and selling efforts are mainly communication platforms for your USP but it is the customer that determines what your company's unique value is based on their perceptions of and experiences with your company.

Apart from Apple's regular advertisement of the iPhone, they also invested in exceptional customer service, and gave customers a well-designed product. Customers had a great experience using their products and that contributed to their perception of the product.

In creating a USP for your business you need to

know what appeals to the people in your market and know what appeals to your customers about your business. It is not necessarily what is different about you as much as what is important to the customers.

You are in business to satisfy your customers not to show off your uniqueness. If your uniqueness is not what a customer needs then it's NOT a selling point to them.

The aim of business is to satisfy a customer for a profit, so find out what is important to your market before developing your USP.

REFLECT & APPLY:

1. Do your customers know your business or product's Unique Selling Proposition?

   _____

   _____

   _____

2. What steps can you take to ingrain your USP in your customers' minds?

   _____

   _____

   _____

CHAPTER 6

KNOW YOUR MARKET

"When you know your audience, your audience knows"
                                              -Unknown

KNOW YOUR MARKET

If your USP must appeal to your market then you need to rightly identify your market.

As a business you must have your own target market; you really are not yet in business without one, because they constitute the people that will patronize your products and services. So who is your target market? Whose problem are you solving?

As a business you need to be clear who you are targeting with your products and services.

So how do you identify your market? Here are a few guides to help you do that;

1. **Know the problems your product/service is solving.**

   For you to start a business you must have a product or service that you offer, right? One of the ways you start identifying your market is to ask what problem your product is solving.

   If you sell wigs for instance, honey, or furniture etc. Ask yourself what benefit the product really offers.

   What benefit do wigs offer?

What problem does wearing wigs solve?

Every good product must meet a need. If you sell pure honey, you need to ask, what need does honey serve? What special benefits does it provide?

Honey is a healthy alternative to sugar, it is rich in several nutrients that helps reduce the risk of type 2 diabetes and heart diseases. It is not only sweet but also medicinal.

So what type of people need this benefit? Who are those more likely to find it very useful?

Who are those who will find wigs very useful and handy? Ladies who like to look good with different hair styles but don't have the time and can't afford to go through the stress of visiting salons regularly to have their hair made, right? So who are those who fall into that category that you know?

What you do is to ask yourself why do women wear wigs and who are those most likely to find wigs useful. They are the ones you target to sell to.

For honey, you target people who will need or appreciate the benefit it offers? Those with diabetic cases, those who want to avoid sugar and are looking for a healthy alternative. Some people also use honey to improve their skin, they are part of your target market.

Every product determines its customers by the kind of problem it solves and the kind of benefit it offers

2. **Identify prospects from your industry**

Another way to determine your target market is to obtain useful information about the industry you are in. If you are a tailor or boutique owner, for instance, you are in the fashion industry, if you sell household electronics you are in the home appliances industry. Your prospects are definitely among the people who patronize that industry, and purchase products from your competitors and other companies operating in that industry.

It is from them that you start narrowing down to those who fit into your target customer profile; and you get to know those who fit that profile majorly by ASKING different customers in your industry questions.

When I opened a Laundry shop some years ago I asked

customers who patronize such firms a number of questions to determine their likes, dislikes, and what was important to them. Their answers served as a guide for me to determine my target market from the numerous customers in the sector, as not every drycleaning customer fit into my buyer (customer) profile.

Part of the objectives of my market survey was to find out if the customers had a need I could meet better or more satisfactorily than the competition. There were lots of customers patronizing other dry-cleaning firms but still had unmet needs that my business was in a better position to meet. I learnt some customers were patronizing some firms mainly because they had not found a better alternative. Some of them fell within my target customer profile.

NOTE: When it comes to obtaining information from prospects remember that your first approach is not to ask them research questions, but to build rapport. When you do not build rapport with prospects they may be reluctant to answer your questions

3. **Identify your most frequent customers:**

   If you are already operating your business, your most frequent customers will very likely be among your target market. They are frequent because they really need and value your products, and they are able to afford them. This is a major characteristic of your target market.

   Your target market are people who need and value your product, and are both willing and able to pay for it. Those who patronize you frequently already have most of these attributes.

   With the three approaches described above, you should be able identify your target market and create a profile of the kind of customers you should be selling to, this is what is called your buyer persona.

REFLECT & APPLY:

Have you clearly identified the right market for your business? If not you can go through this chapter again and carefully follow the steps to become clear about your target market.

_____
_____
_____

CHAPTER 7

DEVELOPING YOUR USP

"It's not just about what you sell; it's about what stands you out"

-Unknown

DEVELOPING YOUR USP

There is a four point framework you can use to create your Unique Selling Proposition, it comes with the acronym ACTS.

1. **Ask your customers questions:**

   Start by asking your customers questions. As stated earlier, your USP must appeal to your customers and prospects. So you need to know what will appeal to them, and you can find out by asking. You see, you will save yourself a lot of headache by just asking people who patronize you or patronize similar products some relevant questions. It's not like an interview or series of exam questions, it may just be in form of a chat.

Find out, what are your customers' most important considerations in buying your products or similar products?

For instance, if you sell Ankara (African prints) fabrics or wrappers, what are the major elements a customer considers when buying these fabrics? Why will a customer prefer to buy wrappers from one store and not another store?

Is it quality, Price, Brand, etc?

Now you are getting information about why customers buy. I know if you ask them further, quality or price may not be the only considerations.

The reason you ask customers questions is to find out their MOTIVE for buying; Their "WHY".

What is important to them? Is it price, Quality, Uniqueness of design, Brand, Location, Customer relation, etc?

NOTE your answers. If this part is well conducted you should be able to know to a great extent what is important to your target customers.

2. **Conduct Competitor inquiry:**

   Know your competitors, and their good points. One of the first things I did when I wanted to start marketing Drycleaning services was to find out the good points of my competitors in Abuja, Nigeria. I knew those who had very sophisticated machines and ambience, I knew those who offered convenient delivery services, and so on.

   In our dynamic business environment, how can you be in business without knowing your competitors? Who are you differentiating yourself from, if you don't know them?

   You must know those who are doing the same business with you, not to fight them, but to differentiate yourself from them, so customers can have a clear choice.

So, what are the good points of your competitors? What do YOU and other customers like about them? Is it their service, the quality of their products, their delivery speed? Etc.

Some of my friends who were also customers told me what they loved about some of my competitors, and I noted them down.

3. **Turn customers' pains to opportunity:**

   Find out customers' pain points. What are customers complaining about? No matter how good the competition is, there are still aspects the customers are not satisfied about.

   Customer dissatisfaction creates business opportunities.

   Some customers told me their dissatisfaction was delay in delivery of their garments, others said prices of the premium dry cleaners were way beyond their budget.

   What are the customers complaining about? You can turn them to your opportunities.

I charged the lowest prices for some months when I set up my Laundry service in Abuja, and it was because of feedback from prospects. It is good to ask questions.

4. Search within:

What is unique about you, and your business? Remember the previous points; you now know what customers want, you also know the good points of your competitors, and the pain points or dissatisfaction of several customers.

So, what is unique about you? There is something unique about everyone, truly.

You need to now dig those special things out. Things that you know will be relevant to your customers.

- What experiences do you have?
- What are your special skills?
- Do you have any relationship with some credible partners (foreign or local)?
- Are you very good in customer relations?
- Do you have lots of relevant qualifications for your line of business?

- Do you have more variety for your product line than your competitors?
- Do you have staff with specialized skills that are relevant to customers?
- Are you fast at delivering your services? Will customers appreciate speed in delivery?
- Is your office or store environment more comfortable and serene for customers than those of competitors?
- Is your cake better decorated than most of your competition?
- Are you very talented in coming up with creative garment designs?
- Do you have a special way of training children that will make them understand faster?

I can go on and on. If you look well you will find.

DIVERSE WAYS TO DIFFERENTIATE YOUR BUSINESS AND OFFERINGS;

1. **Your product:**

    Do you have a unique design? Does it last longer? Does it perform better? Does it have more nutrients? Are they more organic etc?

2. **Service:**

    Are you more courteous, caring, or faster in responding to customers?

3. **Personnel:**
   Do you have experts on your team?

4. **Ambience:**
   Is the atmosphere of your store appealing and welcoming?

5. **Image:**
   Do you have a favourable public perception and image? Do you have a high level of credibility?

Search for the unique points you can find about yourself and your business, and you WILL FIND, if you search well. You will find something special that customers will really like, and competitors do not have, or cannot easily match.

It was a customer that helped me to identify some special attributes of my own business. Sometimes you can't see your own special points, it will take an external party to point out what they like about you or your business. That is why asking customers questions is a VERY good thing.

Our packaging and customer relations were aspects my customers considered special about my Dry-cleaning outfit then. I never knew our customer relations approach was a big deal to our customers, but it was, and that was a good learning point for me.

In a company I once worked with, one of our selling points was our foreign experience and partnership. We often wrote in proposals that our company had consulted in that particular area of business in the United Kingdom and Europe for over 10 years, and we still had our technical partner in Europe. No other company of similar nature I knew in Abuja or its environs then could match that resume. That was a selling point and it made several companies believe in our capacity to deliver results.

If you search well, you will find a selling point you can promote to win in your market. It can even be the story of your business and how it started; maybe something unique and captivating about it. All these can stand you out in the MIND of customers.

So search and you will find.

REFLECT & APPLY:

Have you identified the unique selling points of your business? If not, you can carefully go through the above framework again to ascertain them.

_____

_____

_____

CHAPTER 8

FROM PERSONAL TO CORPORATE

"For better or for worse, our company is a reflection of my thinking, my character, and my values"
-Rupert Murdoch

FROM PERSONAL TO CORPORATE

Do you know many of the great businesses you see today are extensions of the unique talents, personalities, and values of the founders? The founders brought their uniqueness to the business world and expressed them through their companies and their market embraced them.

The Unique typography associated with Apple products was inspired by Steve Job's love for calligraphy. He had learnt calligraphy as a student at Reed Liberal Arts College in Portland Oregon, and he loved it.

Apple products' software is flexible, easy to use and

remains one of their selling points, The software was actually the brain child of the two innovative geniuses who founded the company - Steve Jobs and Steve Wozniak. The founders were great inventors, who were very simple but had good taste, and those attributes were reflected in their product offering.

KFC is known for its unique fried chicken. The uniqueness of its chicken stems from the founder's skill in making chicken with special spices and herbs, the company's unique recipe, coupled with its speed of serving customers have been institutionalized to give it a unique brand.

What is Walmart Stores' unique selling proposition? The company is known around the world for offering goods at "Everyday low price" in all their chains. People walk into a Walmart store knowing they will get goods at the lowest prices, but how did the company come up with this unique edge? It came from the founder's personality and values; Sam Walton was known to keep a tight fist and count his pennies, even after he had achieved great wealth as a result of the success of Walmart he continued to drive his old pickup truck and stay in budget hotel rooms when he travelled on business trips.

He was very good at bargaining prices and preferred to have lower margins and make up for them with higher volume of sales. His so called "stingy" nature helped him to cut costs in the organization and keep expenses low so profit can go up. He often had great ideas of cutting cost and knew how to keep expenses low across board. He decided to incorporate that unique strength or attribute into his business. He also deliberately employed people who were good at managing cost. He successfully institutionalized that approach which has made the company stand out among Retail Chains.

Instead of looking for external ideas first look within. Start with what you have.

Someone once said Richard Branson of Virgin Group is a rock star and entertainer doing business, but that is not the right description. Richard Branson is an entrepreneur who has brought his uniqueness into his business and has succeeded at it, with chains of businesses and a net worth of about $5billion. He possesses an interesting personality that delights in having fun. He has an adventurous streak to him; he is either Kite surfing at Necker Island, or trying to break world record by crossing the Atlantic in a hot air balloon.

He is not your typical CEO, as he can often be found wearing shorts and T-Shirt for work, or sometimes dressed in Zulu outfit for a product launch. He also has a passion for philanthropy.

He shamelessly brought his uniqueness into the running of his businesses and his target market loved it; his unique attributes made him stand out in the markets he played in. He once said "No two successful entrepreneurs are the same. Rather, their different ways of thinking and individuality makes the difference".

By giving expression to your difference you can make your business stand out too.

YOUR UNIQUE STRENGTHS AS YOUR STRATEGIC DIFFERENTIATOR.

Let me explain how your unique, natural strengths can be the differentiator for your own business;

The truth is that we are all created different; and no two human beings are the same – in personality, values, experiences, interests, talents, and in several other respects.

If you and I do the same business we can never do it exactly the same way, there will still be some obvious differences because of our individual uniqueness. So how can you be deliberate in incorporating your unique attributes into your business in such a way that it makes your business a distinctive and appealing brand to a specific market?

Many people do not consciously bring their uniqueness to bear in their businesses; but you should, especially if it is one that will appeal to your market.

As a business owner, you have unique passions, gifts, personal values, a particular set of people you will like to help, and attributes people compliment you on. Besides the fact that you can differentiate your products (i.e. improving quality, changing features, uses etc.), customer service (exceptional customer relations), identity (i.e. your logo), communication (i.e. your advert, messages), and lots more, it is important to know that your innate strengths can serve as major tools for differentiation.

You are already naturally different from other people. You often don't need a complex process to become different. What you need to do is to discover your difference - those unique customer appealing attributes you possess, and highlight them in your business, groom and develop them, make them an integral part of your business, and keep associating your business with them in your marketing communications.

I will give you some examples;

Three friends that graduated from catering school decided to start their own restaurants. They were living in the same city, and did not plan to leave anytime soon. Each one had the dream of starting a restaurant and they decided to go on to actualize their dream.

One of them got a loan from his uncle and started an eatery; the other two used their savings from their previous employment and an SME grant they received to start their restaurants.

The first friend has a unique personality; he is a very organized and detailed person, and a perfectionist. His kind of music is cool and classy. That was his peculiarity.

He went ahead to set up a classy restaurant, well arranged, with good furnishing, chandeliers, excellent interior décor, and strictly jazz music. The waiters were courteous, neatly dressed, and professional.

The restaurant blended with his calm personality, value of excellence, and attention to details, and the elites in the city constituted the bulk of the customers that patronized the restaurant.

The second friend is a jovial, friendly, happy go lucky guy. He set up a restaurant with loud music, pop and rock, the restaurant was always lively, he chatted with almost every customer, and he was very warm and friendly. Many young people loved the eatery. It was very entertaining. The waiters were very friendly; they checked up on the customers, and the eatery services were very flexible, not too organized like that of the first friend.

The selling point of the eatery was the warmth and friendliness customers enjoyed there and the fact that it was entertaining.

It blended with the personality of the owner and it attracted the right kind of customers.

The third friend is a serious, hardworking, result oriented person. He is fast in executing tasks and loves prompt service. He decided to set up a drive-by eatery. Takeout services was a major feature of the eatery; you drive by, place your order, and in few minutes your order is ready. The busy professionals in the city preferred to patronize the eatery.

Each one had his customer base, because of the nature of their restaurants. Each of them infused their values, personalities, and interests into their business. They highlighted what was peculiar about them, and customers who loved that came to them.

An American businessman once told us about his younger brother, who quit his job to become a Financial Adviser to small businesses. When he started the business he discovered there were so many financial advisers already; almost everywhere he went someone will introduce himself as a financial adviser to businesses in one or more sectors. This made him somewhat discouraged; he thought to himself "A lot of people in the city are financial advisers. I am just a rookie here, I don't even stand a chance".

Then someone advised him to search within, and take stock of his talents, passions, values, and interests, and see how he can bring them into his business to differentiate it in the market.

He took a pen and paper, and wrote down as many as he could find, of all the attributes peculiar to him. Then he settled with a few points. He is a sports enthusiast, and he loves the game of basketball so much. He decided to target basketball players and enthusiasts. He surveyed the market and found it viable. Many in the sports arena and especially basketball players needed financial advisers, and people to manage their money for them. A number of them were rich and careless with their spending, and because of his love for the game of basketball, the people in that industry were very comfortable with him.

He could chat with them for hours about basketball, and he could watch games and competitions together with them. They thus allowed him to consult for them. He was the financial adviser they trusted more, because they believed he had their interest at heart.

He soon became popular as a financial adviser to many sports personalities.

How did he breakthrough in that industry? He looked within. He found his difference and capitalized on it.

I have been invited to speak in a few forums; I remember last year at a particular forum where I was among the speakers on a particular topic. I noticed something that day; after giving my talk, many of those who greeted me said they were inspired by it. Some said they felt encouraged, another person said he was motivated to do more with his life.

I thanked all of them for the feedback. Feedbacks are always very important.

Another speaker spoke on the same topic; he was very good at reeling out statistics, and quoting figures to support his points. I remember him quoting World Bank statistics on poverty and others. He reeled out statistics by heart and used logic and references to back up his claims. He got a good applause from the audience as well, and people asked him for further help in Development analysis.

The third speaker, I still remember him very well. The moment he got on stage to speak, within three minutes many people were laughing, some were reeling with laughter on their seats.

He was so funny! He is naturally humorous; we laughed till the end of the speech.

Every one of us spoke well that day I must say, but we each brought our uniqueness into the presentations. And those who loved what we stood for and what we offered came looking for us after the speech.

I noticed again that day that we are all different. We just need to take the time to look within for our difference.

Get a paper and pen. Write all you know about yourself that makes you unique and different; your vision, your values, your personality, your talents, your passion, your experiences, your professional track records, what customers compliment you on, your style, your hobbies, your interests, etc. Write as many as you can remember.

Then think of two or three points or aspects you can incorporate into your business. Make sure it is something that will appeal to the customers you are targeting.

If you incorporate a strength that comes naturally to you into your business it will be easy for you to sustain it. After infusing it into your business, ensure you promote it effectively to your market.

I know a lady who runs a Startup in the ladies fashion industry; her selling point is her attention to details and network of relationships with elites in her city. She carved a niche for herself based on her natural social circle and sold her products at a premium, because her customers value excellent details in their garments.

I know one of her competitors in business whose selling point is exceptional customer relations skills; she is very courteous, and overly customer sensitive. She beats her competitors in this regard. She is always top of mind to her customers. Her strength is natural, and she has institutionalized it in her company. Excellent customer relations, according to her own style and values, is what her company is now known for.

Find your difference, and highlight it, promote it, and stand out in your market.

REFLECT & APPLY:

As the owner or CEO of your business which of your unique attributes, passions, philosophies, and experiences can you bring to bear and incorporate into your business to make it unique?

_____
_____
_____

CHAPTER 9

FROM INNATE VIRTUE TO BUSINESS VALUE

What sets you apart….a lot of the time is what makes you great

-Emma Stone

FROM INNATE VIRTUE TO BUSINESS VALUE

Some time ago, I was resident in a large estate for more than six years. The estate had a mixture of quiet neighbourhoods and commercial centres with several malls, grocery stores and small businesses. There was a barber's shop within my neighborhood which had a reputation for cleanliness. I loved going to cut my hair at that salon, and so did several other customers because of their spick-and-span ambience. Many people came from other parts of the estate to patronize this particular shop as well. Even though there were several other barber shops located all around the estate, this shop stood out because of its special appeal, and it has maintained this competitive edge for over ten years.

Here is what I found out from my experience at the shop and interaction with the staff;

The founder's virtue

The owner of the shop had worked as a Cashier in a company for several years before starting the barbing business in the neighbourhood. Many of his colleagues refer to him as Mr. Clean because of his passion for cleanliness. He was said to be difficult to please with regards to sanitation of his office environment, as he often complained that the janitors were not cleaning well enough. Time and time again, he cleaned his office space even after the janitor had done the regular morning cleaning. There were times he arranged the entire office himself even though that was not his job, and everyone could clearly see the difference when he was done. He indeed had an innate passion for spotless workspaces, and he brought that virtue to bear in his business; not with the intention to create a competitive edge, but to create an environment he was comfortable in.

The Standard

The owner was not only passionate about neatness; he made it a standard practice in his shop. He taught his barbers how to clean the shop and maintain a hygienic environment, and he emphasized the need for staff to look neat at all times. They had a morning cleaning routine in the shop, and I noticed the barbers were regularly keeping the shop tidy throughout the day. On some days, the owner (who I refer to as Mr. Clean) would show up at the shop, and if he is unsatisfied with the level of cleanliness, he would grab the cleaning tools, roll up his sleeves and get to work cleaning the whole place. After a while, most of the staff learnt from his example, and to a large extent started maintaining the same hygienic standards.

I also noticed that every new staff imbibed the neatness culture without any formal induction Within a few days of resumption, they just got to know that it was a 'grave sin' not to maintain the spick-and-span ambience of the shop.

The monitoring

The shop was managed by Mr. Clean's cousin who I noticed clearly shared his value for cleanliness. I have heard him emphasize the importance of cleanliness severally to the staff and seen him clean the place a couple of times. Every staff knows that anytime the owner comes to the shop the first thing he checks is the neatness of the place, from the floor to the odour of the store and the neatness of the staff. None of them wanted to be in his 'dirty books'; they all made his priority their priority as well.

The result of infusing his personal values in the business, setting a standard, and implementing appropriate monitoring mechanisms was a business that stood out in its market with a unique competitive edge. I noticed a number of more sophisticated competitors found it difficult to maintain such a standard because it was not a major value or culture for them and it was not driven with passion from the management as in the case of 'Mr. Clean's business.

LESSONS FROM MR. CLEAN' BARBER'S SHOP

I saw how 'Mr. Clean's' personal virtue became his business' unique selling point because he successfully institutionalized it. His approach is what every small business owner can learn from. The following are the lessons from it;

1. **Instill your values in your team:** This is done by training your staff, promoting and getting buy-in, and exemplifying the value as the leader and major driver of your organizational culture.

2. **Institutionalize your value in the business:** You need to document that virtue as a core value to be practiced in your organization; develop a standard procedure for practicing it, just as Mr. Clean did this by instituting a morning cleaning routine in his shop. If you want to institutionalize a learning, teamwork, excellence, or fun culture in your company, you need to have spelt out processes staff can follow to achieve them. You also need to set up a structure that will provide an enabling environment for its implementation. For instance, to engender excellence in your company, you must have quality standards in your departments based on best practices and ensure staff performance are regularly measured against those standards. The leadership should set up business sessions where global standards are assessed and staff are motivated to exceed them. If you want fun to be institutionalized in your company you can have Fridays set aside as special fun days, create time for music and jokes, your office walls can have witty quotes, and you could develop a calendar of entertaining events throughout the year.

3. **Regularly monitor to ensure the values are kept:** It is important to assess the staff, structure, and practices in your organization from time to time to ensure that your

major values are still being kept. Let adherence to the values be part of your recruitment criteria as well as your staff performance assessment criteria. When rewards and penalties are attached to compliance or non-compliance with those values they will be taken more seriously by the staff. Positive motivation like recognition, appreciation, and promotion will encourage more compliance. Above all, effective monitoring and evaluation will enable you identify gaps in your staff and organization that can be addressed with more knowledge and education about the values.

4. **As the leader you must be passionate about the value for it to stand out in your organization:** Strong organizational values and cultures are built by passionate and exemplary leadership. Both the leader and his team must be passionate about it, and this comes through regular sensitization, education/training and accrued benefits of practicing those values.

It was difficult for the competitors to match the competitive edge of "Mr. Clean's" barber shop because they were not as passionate about cleanliness as he was and they were not keen on paying the price of commitment and persistence required to sustain that unique value.

It is difficult for competitors to imitate your unique selling point if you and your organization are really passionate about it and have embraced it as a major value. And if you, as the business leader, are a 'natural' with that unique selling point you will be several steps ahead of those who are merely imitating because both passion and instincts will work naturally to your advantage.

I learnt from Mr. Clean's barber's shop that an enduring unique selling point requires more than frequent advertisement and a documented service policy for the company; it must be passionately emphasized and exemplified by the company leadership.

REFLECT & APPLY:

What steps can you take to institutionalize your unique or special personal virtues and values in your company?

_____

_____

_____

CHAPTER 10

PROMOTING YOUR USP

"It's not what you sell that matters as much as how you sell it"

-Brian Halligan

PROMOTING YOUR USP

Knowing your unique strengths and incorporating them into your business will give your business a unique identity; but that identity has to be promoted to the right market. The benefits of your USP need to be effectively communicated to your audience. Don't just tell customers how great you are as a business or how great your products are; tell them what is in it for them, what your products will do for them, and what they will benefit from patronizing your business. Benefit sells.

Let's use the pure honey business as a quick case study; after you have identified what is unique about the business or product, which may be the quality (i.e. purity of the honey), the company's customer service skills, prompt delivery process etc. the next step is to promote it. You can even start by giving the product a name to project the value you want to promote. You could name it Proven pure honey, for instance, if the unadultrated quality is its major selling point. Then go ahead to state what it will it do for customers. State the benefits the unique value i.e purity of the honey will deliver to buyers.

Once you've identified what is unique and market relevant about your business, ensure you PROMOTE it well. Promoting it well includes sharing the message and stories your audience can connect with, and using the right channels, online or offline, to reach your target market.

When I noticed that customers in my neighborhood, who were part of my target market, were price sensitive, I came up with a unique pricing model for them while still offering quality service with good packaging. This made my offer very attractive to them and several of my customers. They were pleased to get such qualitative service at a flexible and affordable rate. The promotional phrase for my business then was "Look good at a good margin", and this resonated with a lot of my target market. My marketing message was coined based on the feedback I got from my market survey.

It's always important to obtain valid information about the needs, preferences, and pain points of your market; that is the information you use to plan your marketing strategy.

My message communicated to my target customers, who were largely young average income professionals, that they could still regularly look good and smart on a favourable budget. That was a hit with many of them.

REFLECT & APPLY:

1. Are you promoting your USP well? Are you communicating the right message, benefits, and stories using the appropriate channel for your target customers?

   _____
   _____
   _____

2. If not, what can you do to improve on your promotion?

   _____
   _____
   _____

CHAPTER 11

CRAFTING YOUR USP IN THE MIND

"Products are made in the factory but brands are created in the mind"

-Walter Landor

CRAFTING YOUR USP IN THE MIND

Your Unique Selling Point is only effective when it is well built and positioned in the customers' MINDS. A good USP is one that your market acknowledges and constantly attributes to you.

HOW TO BUILD YOUR USP IN CUSTOMERS' MINDS

To effectively build your USP in your customers' (and prospects') minds ensure the following;

1. **Positive customer experiences:** Customers' experiences with your products, your services, and your staff can reinforce or erode your Unique Selling Point in their minds.

   So you have to ensure your products deliver what you promised it will. Keep your customer experiences positive and in line with your promised USP always.

2. **Promote your Unique Selling Point:** SHOUT it aloud that you have proven pure honey, unique and top quality Ankara fabrics, a transformational coaching program, or an affordable grocery store, for instance; so that those who really want it will find their way to your door step.

   What is the use of a Unique Selling Point if people do not know about it? So use the right channels for your target market to promote your unique edge and benefits.

3. **Do it consistently:** That is, you should do it frequently, and also make sure it's a similar message customers get all the time.

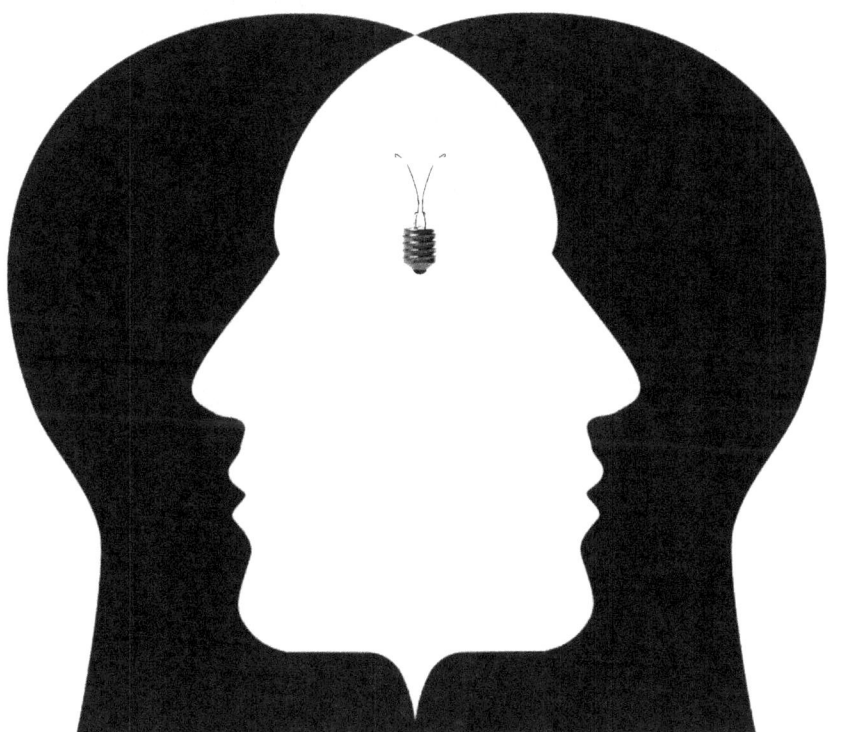

USP is retained in customers' minds through consistent communication. Say the same thing in different ways very frequently and customers will identify your business with that. Say it on your website, your social media platforms, your physical store, your products, through your salespersons, your fliers, brochures etc. let it be a consistent message on all your channels and customer touch points (where customers interface with you).

Consistency reinforces your USP and makes customers remember your business easily, identify it, and differentiate it from the competition. Your business becomes a clear choice in their minds.

REFLECT & APPLY:

1. Are your customer experiences with your business consistent with the values you promote about it? If not, how can you correct that?

   _____
   _____
   _____

2. What steps can you take to ensure consistency in communicating your USP?

   _____
   _____
   _____

CHAPTER 12

THERE IS NO COMPETITION

Authenticity can't be replicated or faked. You're either real or you're not.

-Bibi Bourelly

If any of you lacks wisdom, let him ask God

-James 1:5

THERE IS NO COMPETITION

I got the inspiration to write this chapter, after I thought I had finished writing this book. I literally jumped out of bed to pen this down so I do not lose the flow of inspiration.

I will share two exceptional ways to enable you stand out in your market effectively. These strategies will put you in a class of your own and ahead of the competition in your marketplace.

The first time I really understood these methods was about a year ago, after an experience I had with some members of my online business community. I was reading a book sometime in September 2019 when I got an inspiration to start an online community of small business entrepreneurs and leaders. The aim was to train, coach and support them to grow their businesses successfully. Initially, I was hesitant to follow through with this idea. I doubted my readiness and capacity to lead a community of entrepreneurs. I had observed the work of some coaches that I admire and felt I could not measure up to their standards at the moment. I also felt that the Small and Medium Scale Enterprise market was saturated with several coaches, trainers and consultants offering similar services to the same audience, so I thought of playing in a different market to make a good break. However, I could not let go of the thought. About one month later, precisely on 15th October 2019, after one of my online trainings, I announced to my participants that I was opening a forum for an online community for small business owners and asked if they would like to join. Many of them indicated interest and quickly joined with the link I created. Fourteen of them joined the group, I was the fifteenth member and I added my wife to make a total of sixteen founding members.

We started with regular weekend trainings, business clinics and some one-on-one sessions based on request. At that time, I felt comfortable with managing a small group. I just wanted to develop the capacity of members, using my knowledge base. My training approach was basic, I posted texts and voice notes on the WhatsApp group, but the feedback and testimonials I received from members were amazing. So I kept at it.

In January 2020, there was a global outbreak of COVID-19 and by March of the same year we had a government imposed lockdown that kept me home with my family like several other people across the world. During this period, I had ample time so I used the opportunity to embark on more research about emerging trends and engaged the community with different training sessions. I saw the group grow exponentially within this period, without any major advertisement and it started demanding more of my attention and commitment. We even had to move to Telegram platform for better engagement. A few months later, the community grew beyond a thousand three hundred (1,300) members both within and outside my country. I also kept receiving encouraging feedback about the impact of our sessions on the lives of members and their businesses as more of them got practical strategies, ideas and support to grow their businesses.

The two major lessons I got from this experience were to listen to my inner voice more and be confident enough to be myself and use what works for me. These are two powerful keys that helped me grow and impact the community. They have also been helpful in different aspects of my life and business.

Let me explain these keys a bit more:

1. **Be unapologetically authentic:**

   Over the years, many of us have heard that "no two human beings are the same". We all have unique DNAs, fingerprints and voices amongst others. Our physical, mental and emotional attributes are all unique to each one of us, including our temperaments and personalities.

   This is common knowledge, but the problem is that many of us are still unable to be ourselves and express our uniqueness. We have this constant battle within ourselves which often undermines our capacity to own and be proud of our unique identity. We tend to conform to a mold sold to us by the society, press or religion as the case may be.

   Some of the factors aiding the loss of our uniqueness can include our families, peers and also the school system. My younger brother was left-handed while growing up and he was often taunted by some of our relatives for being a 'lefty', because they thought it was abnormal to be left-handed. I am grateful my parents let him be himself. He would have been pressured to change out of shame. That is how early our identities can start getting compromised.

You may have faced pressure to build a career in a pensionable 9 to 5 job rather than take the risk to become a serial entrepreneur that you believe you are. You may have encountered pressure from your peers to socialize a lot more, be a night crawler and more adventurous when you know you are a lot happier living a quiet and studious life. You may be under pressure from your religious association to always wear a suit and tie for your teaching and speaking engagements when you naturally feel more relaxed wearing a shirt with a pair of chinos and sneakers. (I know you can always dress to suit the requirements of your workplace, customers or audience; these are exceptional situations though).

You may have noticed the way business coaches market their products online, even though you keep getting ideas on how to use a different approach to market your business, but you ignore your 'strange' ideas to follow the popular methods.

Many people find it hard to be themselves because of

the need for societal acceptance. John Mason once said that "the opposite of courage is conformity". When you overcome the fear of societal acceptance you can stand out from the crowd.

The common statement "Be yourself" is about the most difficult one to adhere to, largely because of the fear of criticism and societal rejection. Most times what we call the norm in our society will only box us in and stifle the expression of our uniqueness. I am convinced that everyone, including entrepreneurs and business leaders, can stand out in their sphere of endeavor if they become unapologetically authentic. While I believe in personal growth and development, its purpose is not to change our identity but to enhance it, so it is important to avoid embracing external ideas and concepts to the detriment of your idiosyncrasies in the name of personal improvement and change. Your aim should be to refine your raw peculiarities through training and then manifest them.

As an entrepreneur, you have a unique identity, which includes your set of values, talents, strengths, personality and life experiences. These elements should rub off on your business to make it different from others. The same way warmth and human connection can be associated with Starbucks, you can have your personal values reflected in your business too. Sharing your personal story as the founder or your startup experience may be what attracts you to your target market. You may prefer a different method of marketing your services to your audience; you may be inclined to use music and entertainment on social media to push your brand, give inspiring talks, or simply use written poems to market your services. You may choose not to use the conventional social media channels, but engage in real life conversations to get customers. The point is to be courageous enough to carry out your inclinations and be yourself once you find what works for you.

When you start sharing your unique story unapologetically, communicating your message and the solution you offer your market, you will start attracting your own clients – those who find your style attractive and impactful.

It is so hard to replicate an authentic identity. You are in a class of your own in that space. For some people, the problem is that you have not started shinning your own light, because when you burn with your own unique fire you will attract the people you are meant to serve. Your vibe will always attract your tribe.

So look within, awaken and manifest your authenticity in your business. I know you can be anything you want to be in life, as some will often say, but the best decision you can make is to choose to be YOU and let that reflect in your business.

REFLECT & APPLY:

1. Do you know your authentic self (identity), or has it been subsumed over the years?

   _____

   _____

   _____

2. Take some time alone to reflect, uncover and take note of your natural talents, passion, values and unique experiences that have shaped your life for good.

   _____

   _____

   _____

3. Start giving expression to what you discover to be your unique values, talents, story, message to the world etc. and take little bold steps to implement those compelling ideas you have about your business.

   _____

   _____

   _____

2. **Listen to your inner voice:**

There is another source of knowledge beyond the conventional books, seminars and discussions with people. Many of us have acquired knowledge from this source, albeit accidentally but definitely not through a deliberate process.

Many of the ideas that have significantly changed our world are from this source and some of the legendary personalities we admire (dead or alive), have trusted this source for their choice information and ideas.

Over the years, this peculiar source has been called different names, some call it intuition, others call it sixth sense, clairvoyance, epiphany or inspiration. Most times when people say they had a light bulb moment while taking a shower or a sudden burst of inspiration while taking an evening walk, that is what they are referring to. This is a unique source of information or wisdom that can help you solve some significant problems or excel in an endeavor.

What happened to Isaac Newton when he was hit on the head by an apple while sitting under an apple tree alone?

He simply had an "aha" moment and it triggered the discovery of the law of gravity, which has changed the way we understand the universe today.

Some of the greatest discoveries of mankind as well as ideas that have revolutionized industries and markets did not emanate from conventional sources like books and academic lectures, but came through this higher dimension of knowledge. I like a popular quote by Albert Einstein, which says "the intuitive mind is a sacred gift and the rational mind is a faithful servant". Many people would naturally assume Einstein was more scientific and logical in his decision-making, but this quote proves otherwise. He understood the value of the intuitive mind.

We can all have regular access to this source of information if we know how to cultivate the discipline it requires. The intuitive mind will generate ideas and strategies that are unique to you and your business. Your competitors will be unable to get these strategies because they are not commonly available. Implementing those ideas will often make you stand out in your marketplace.

The truth is that most of the intuitive knowledge people access, are just bits of wisdom from God, freely given for human beings to succeed in their endeavours and implement His plans on the earth. You can have direct access to that superior and exclusive wisdom through a relationship with God. He will give you insights that are unique to you and your business. If you are bold enough to carry them out, you will be distinguished in your market and operate your business in unique ways that your market cannot help but notice. Customers will know that they are getting a value from you that they cannot get elsewhere, not necessarily because the value is better (which can also be the case) but because it is different. Only God's wisdom can give you that unique signature, because He created you and designed a unique vision for your work and business as well.

Shae Bynes, the founder of Kingdom Driven Entrepreneur community, which I was also a part of, often shares her story on how she set up the pricing for her Firestarter Online school. The school teaches entrepreneurs how to work out their businesses in partnership with God. After taking the time to develop the entire course content and translating it into an online program, she decided to pray and ask God for a strategy to price and launch it. She shared that God spoke to her heart and told her to launch it at a pay-as-you-choose price. This sounded ludicrous to her, but she had learnt to be radically obedient to His voice. She did as she was led and reaped a huge harvest from that decision. Customers have paid from 25 Cents to over a thousand dollars for the online school and several thousands have been impacted by it. Many people got to hear about the Kingdom Driven Entrepreneur movement through the Firestarter school and have gone ahead to join the community. Besides, that decision has also earned profitable income for the organization.

I had a similar experience at an online strategy session with some entrepreneurs from different parts of the world. A few days before the planned session, I discussed with some of the participants concerning the challenges they encountered in their businesses and I found their challenges quite complicated. I could not figure out a good solution even after studying about the issues. Up until a few hours to the strategy session I was still pondering on what to say to them.

Exactly one hour before the session, I decided to spend some time in quiet meditation, praying in the Spirit and seeking for a higher dimension of wisdom from God. Within that time I got some unique insights for each of them, which I shared at the strategy session. It was indeed a breakthrough moment for them as they all got a clear road-map out of their business challenges. They were also intrigued at the way I approached their issues. I received a unique problem-solving approach to use for them, not from a book, seminar or even my memory, but from within, through the Spirit of God. I have used this same approach a number of times to prepare for corporate trainings, examinations and brainstorming sessions amongst others. I am also using it to write this book.

God's Spirit is the most excellent source of wisdom for you to excel and profit in your business. I have seen some strange but exceptional results from applying this wisdom in my professional life, marriage and other relationships. I cannot think of a better way to stand out in your business than cultivating the discipline to regularly access this wisdom, which comes from within you, if you have a relationship with God.

"I am the LORD your God, Who teaches you to profit, Who leads you by the way you should go" Isaiah 48:17

REFLECT & APPLY:

If you want to cultivate the discipline to regularly access unique divine wisdom and insights for your business, it starts with a relationship with God.

Meditate on this scripture and ask God to give you understanding;

"Are you tired? Worn out? Burned out on religion? Come to me. Get away with me and you'll recover your life. I'll show you how to take a real rest. Walk with me and work with me – watch how I do it. Learn the unforced rhythms of grace. I won't lay anything heavy or ill-fitting on you. Keep company with me and you'll learn to live freely and lightly" Matthew 11:28-30 (MSG).

CHAPTER 13

SHINE YOUR LIGHT

"And who would light a lamp and then hide it in an obscure place? Instead, it's placed where everyone in the house can benefit from its light"

-Matthew 5:15 (TPT)

SHINE YOUR LIGHT

We are at a time when solutions are needed in different spheres of human life and the society. People wake up every day looking for unique solutions to their specific problems and challenges.

I believe there is a solution somewhere for every problem that exists in the market place. More often than not the solutions are with different individuals, some of whom are yet to discover and start giving expression to them. Some of the markets that seem saturated and industries currently experiencing a lull are so because there is no innovation from market players including new entrants.

There is really no saturated market, where demand has gone flat and there is no longer potential for growth. Consumers in such markets are just waiting for innovation; a company that can bring an original idea that will meet a specific need in the market. Consumers will readily embrace any business that offers a creative solution, something different from the 'same old'.

The business environment needs individuals who are creative and courageous enough to be themselves and express their uniqueness through their businesses in the industries they belong. Most business owners have the potential to stand out in their markets if only they can discover their uniqueness, express them, incorporate them into their businesses, and promote them to the right market.

As an entrepreneur or intending business owner you need to go beyond imitation, or just following the trend in your market. You want to shine your light, and bring your authenticity into play. You want to create from within you the unique solutions you have for people, and look for a viable market for the solutions you offer. Your market is waiting for you to shine your light. As Howard Truman rightly said "Do not ask what the world needs. Ask what makes you come alive, and go do it. Because what the world needs are people who have come alive".

And really, the world is waiting for you, and your business to truly come alive.

REFLECT & APPLY:

What are the two major steps you can start taking for you and/or your business to TRULY come alive?

_____

_____

_____

I hope you enjoyed reading this book. Take action on what you have learnt in order to see the results you desire.

For subsequent editions and other new books by Opeyemi Abe visit
www.opeyemiabe.com

www.ingramcontent.com/pod-product-compliance
Lightning Source LLC
Chambersburg PA
CBHW052324220526
45472CB00001B/260